Volleyball Coloring Book & More

Coloring pages, activities, and creative space for players & fans!

Cora Delmonico

We suggest you use crayons, colored pencils or gel pens for the coloring pages. Markers might seep through. If you want to use markers, put a piece of paper in between pages.

Dedicated to Carly, my favorite player.

Tournament Scavenger Hunt

Do on your own or form a small team to compete!

Find as many items on the list as you can in one tournament. Try not to use anyone from your own team & be honest!

- A team wearing red jerseys
- Popcorn on the floor
- Someone wearing a hat
- Diet Soda
- White knee pads
- A team with matching shoes
- A player with the number 18
- A hairbrush
- Someone wearing purple nail polish
- Someone crying
- A kid playing on their phone
- An empty toilet paper roll
- A girl with a white headband
- A fan in your team's tee shirt!
- A left handed player
- A blue gear bag
- Someone wearing a jersey from a different sport
- A coach eating a hot dog or nachos
- Someone dancing
- A purple water bottle
- A baby or toddler
- Grandparents
- A book
- A drinking fountain
- The bracket for this tournament
- A whistle that is NOT silver or black
- Something rainbow colored
- A player with short hair
- A team wearing sleeveless jerseys
- Someone with a broken bone
- A cooler
- Sunglasses
- A messy table
- A shirt representing the city you are in (a team, school, landmark)
- A broom
- A ball other than a volleyball
- Something from behind the bleachers or under a chair
- A plastic sack
- A tie dyed shirt
- A menu
- The letter F

What are some of your volleyball accomplishments?

Volleyball Smarts

Find the match!

A. Setter
B. Libero
C. Outside
D. Right side
E. Middle
F. Defensive specialist
G. Opposite

1. Positions themself on the left front for big hits!
2. Most likely to be involved in every offensive play.
3. Back row player. Wears the same jersey as everyone else.
4. Having a lefty here can be a big advantage.
5. Usually an all around player.
6. Main blocker in the front row.
7. Wears a different colored jersey.

Answers on page 79

Make good habits and they will make you.

Goals

It's always good to have goals. What are some of yours? Put them on this page— they don't have to be volleyball related!

Did you know?
If you write your goals down, you're more likely to achieve them?

Crossword Clues

Across

2. Passing a ball that was an attack from the other side.
4. A serve that doesn't spin.
7. A one handed defensive move where the player is flat on the ground with her hand extended.
11. The best sport!
15. Another name for spiker or attacker.
16. A ball that is returned via bump.
18. Stops an attack!
19. Best of three or best of five wins the _____.

Down

1. Usually the tallest player on the team!
3. A set delivered behind the setter.
5. The vertical rods on the end of the net.
6. Put the ball into play. Done from the back corner of the court.
7. Usually a warm up drill. Also the opposite of salt.
8. A serve that goes over, inbounds, and is not returned.
9. A hit ball that crosses the net and touches the floor.
10. Another name for a bump.
12. The person who wears a different colored shirt.
13. The player who puts the ball into position for a hitter.
14. When the ball doesn't quite make it over the net on a serve, it's _____.
17. The action of hitting the ball.

Crossword Puzzle

Answers on page 81

LOVE

Word Search

```
O U N Q D R Y M V A S R P A K
V R K F E G A H O K P E P P S
Z M E T M T O B L L I G Q W F
I I T B C J C V L R K Y Y W C
N I S H I A N S E A E R P V X
H K F E O L F J Y P O I N T S
Y T O S R A J O B P W R O E U
E J Y D E V M O A H M S L U K
D U J H T W E O L G I D B I F
T W F C T Q R L L D P X B A Z
Q P R L E J H A E H D Y D U K
C C W K S V D O E S N E F E D
I R G P H A U T P U L D Q O R
F O J K K T V J O C U N Y K Q
V W I D F Q S X Y I F A J Z O
```

Defense
Hitter
Libero
Match
Points

Serve
Setter
Sideout
Spike
Volleyball

Answers on page 79

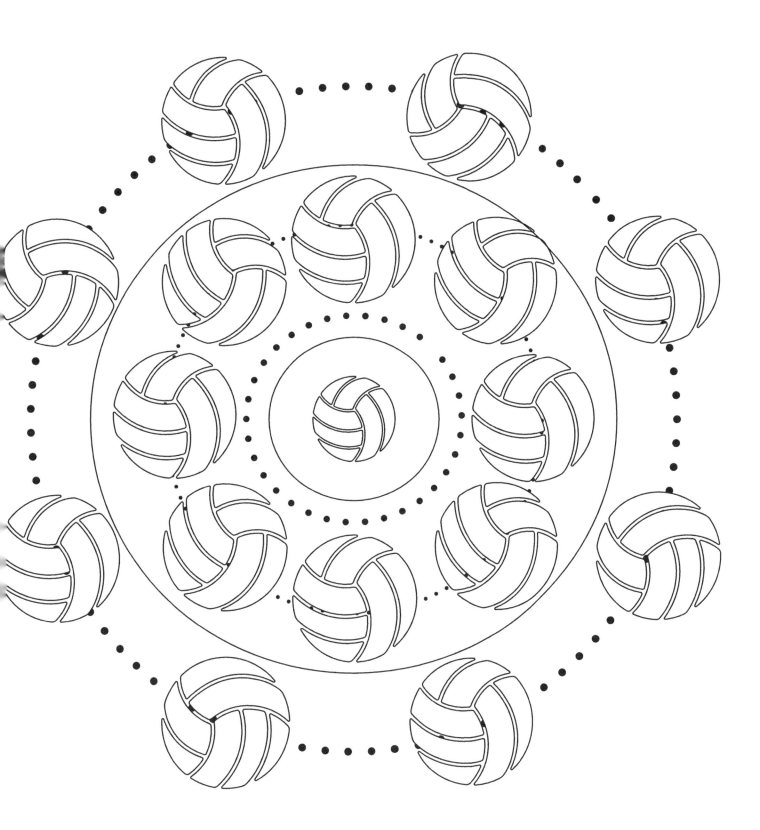

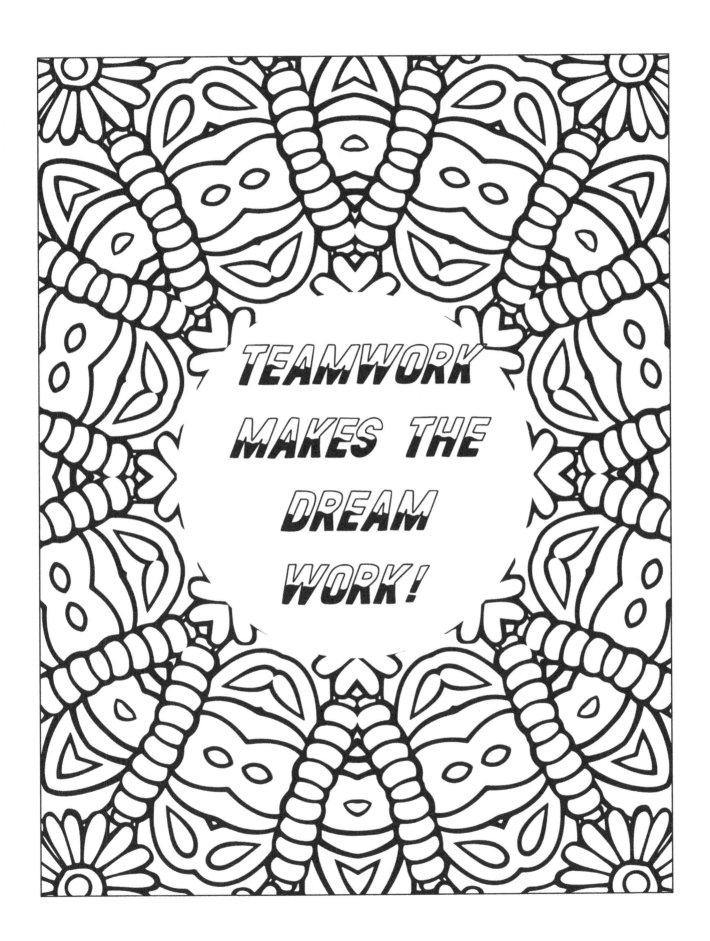

Volleyball Memories

Volleyball

Is My Favorite Season

This Princess won't miss the ball!

A LOOK INSIDE

My Head

VOLLEY BOOM!

Doodle, Draw, Write, Create!

Doodle, Draw, Write, Create!

Doodle, Draw, Write, Create!

Doodle, Draw, Write, Create!

Doodle, Draw, Write, Create!

Doodle, Draw, Write, Create!

Word Search Answers

Volleyball Smarts Answers
A2, B7, C1, D4, E6, F3, G5

Crossword Puzzle Answers

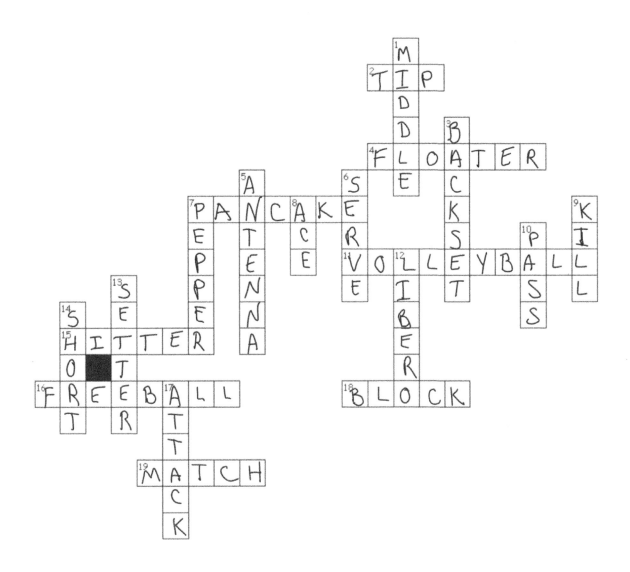

Hey you!
If you want to use markers, tear this page out carefully and put it in between your picture and the next page. It'll stop the marker from leaking through.

Tuck it in this book and use it again & again!

Made in the USA
Monee, IL
11 September 2020